Meet my neighbor, the hair stylist

Marc Crabtree

Author and Photographer

🌲 Crabtree Publishing Company

www.crabtreebooks.com

Crabtree Publishing Company

Meet my neighbor, the hair stylist

To Christine and her talented and friendly family

Author and Photographer
Marc Crabtree

Editor
Reagan Miller

Proofreaders
Corey Long
Crystal Sikkens

Design
Samantha Crabtree

Production coordinator
Margaret Amy Salter

Photographs
All photographs by Marc Crabtree except:
Shutterstock: pages 3, 24 (except makeup artist)

Library and Archives Canada Cataloguing in Publication

Crabtree, Marc
    Meet my neighbor, the hair stylist / Marc Crabtree, author and photographer.

(Meet my neighbor)
ISBN 978-0-7787-4574-7 (bound).--ISBN 978-0-7787-4584-6 (pbk.)

    1. Gomes, Christina--Juvenile literature. 2. Beauty operators--Canada--Biography--Juvenile literature. 3. Hairdressing--Juvenile literature. I. Title. II. Series: Crabtree, Marc. Meet my neighbor.

TT955.G64C73 2010   j646.7'24092   C2009-906786-2

Library of Congress Cataloging-in-Publication Data

Crabtree, Marc.
 Meet my neighbor, the hair stylist / author and photographer Marc Crabtree.
    p. cm. -- (Meet my neighbor)
 ISBN 978-0-7787-4584-6 (pbk. : alk. paper) --
 ISBN 978-0-7787-4574-7 (reinforced library binding : alk. paper)
 1. Beauty operators--Juvenile literature. 2. Hairdressing--Juvenile literature. I. Title. II. Series.

TT958.C73 2010
646.7'24068--dc22

                                                2009047086

Crabtree Publishing Company

www.crabtreebooks.com   1-800-387-7650

Printed in the USA/122009/CG20091120

Published in Canada
Crabtree Publishing
616 Welland Ave.
St. Catharines, Ontario
L2M 5V6

Published in the United States
Crabtree Publishing
PMB 59051
350 Fifth Avenue, 59th Floor
New York, New York 10118

Published in the United Kingdom
Crabtree Publishing
Maritime House
Basin Road North, Hove
BN41 1WR

Published in Australia
Crabtree Publishing
386 Mt. Alexander Rd.
Ascot Vale (Melbourne)
VIC 3032

Meet my Neighbor

Contents

Meet my neighbor, Christine Gomes. Christine is a hair stylist. She lives with her daughter, her sister, her nephew, and her brother.

6

Christine works at her family's beauty salon. She works with her father, her brother, her sister, and their two friends, Tracy and Jennifer.

Christine uses a **flat iron** to straighten this woman's hair.

Jennifer uses a **curling iron** to curl this woman's hair.

Christine helps Jennifer style the woman's long hair.

10

11

Christine talks on the telephone with someone who would like a haircut.

Christine sweeps the floor to pick up all the hair she has cut.

13

Tracy uses **hair spray** to hold this woman's hair in place.

This woman is having her hair styled. She is getting ready for her sister's wedding.

16

Denise is Christine's sister. She is the salon's **makeup artist**. She is putting makeup on this woman.

Christine and Denise have helped these two sisters get ready for the wedding. They are both very happy with their hairstyles and makeup.

Christine uses special brushes and dye to color this woman's hair.

20

She **highlights** the woman's hair from dark brown to light brown.

21

These women are getting ready for a fashion show.

Christine and her co-workers help them style their hair and put on their makeup.

Glossary

flat iron

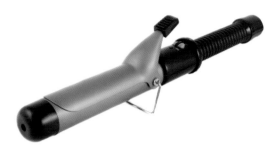

curling iron

hair spray

makeup artist

highlights

Printed in the U.S.A. - CG